EDITED BY JOHN REEVE

LIVING ARTS OF
JAPAN

Published for the Trustees of the British Museum by
British Museum Publications

*This book has been
supported by a
generous donation from*
**The Pilkington
Anglo-Japanese
Cultural Foundation**

© 1990 The Trustees of the British Museum
Published by British Museum Publications Ltd
46 Bloomsbury Street, London WC1B 3QQ
ISBN 0-7141-1445-6
Designed and set by Roger Davies
Printed in Italy by Arti Grafiche Motta

*All the objects illustrated are in the
British Museum unless otherwise stated.*

Previous page Cherry blossom in the
Ueno Park, Tokyo, with the pagoda of
the Toshogu Shrine.

Below Samurai and retainer.
19th-century ornament in coloured
metal inlay on copper.

PREFACE

The idea for this book arose from
Brian Pilkington's generous offer of
support for educational work to take
advantage of the new Japanese
galleries opening at the British
Museum in 1990. After discussions,
particularly with art and design
teachers, the concept of the present
book emerged: to make accessible
some of the key examples of Japanese
art and culture from the British
Museum's collections, with
background information. It is
intended for use in secondary schools
and art colleges, but also by interested
adults, as an introduction to the
temporary exhibitions in the new
galleries, which also include a tea
house donated and built by the
Urasenke Foundation, and a
permanent display of miniature arts
such as *netsuke*, also funded by Mr
and Mrs Pilkington.   Inevitably, the
main problem has been what to leave
out from such a rich collection. The
text concentrates on areas most
requested by teachers: prints, ceramics
and textiles, and themes illustrated by
them, such as theatre, martial arts and
nature. Some of the text is based on
British Museum publications by
Lawrence Smith (Keeper of the
Department of Japanese Antiquities),
Jack Hillier and Victor Harris. I am
especially grateful for the help of
members of the Japanese Department,
in particular Greg Irvine who has
contributed encouragement and
suggestions as well as the section on
origami and some of the photographs.
Photography of British Museum
objects is by members of the British
Museum Photographic Service. Other
photographs are acknowledged on
page 64. This book would not have
been possible without the assistance
of Pat Terry in the Education Service
and the patience, tact and
encouragement of Teresa Francis at
British Museum Publications. Its style
and appearance owe everything to
Roger Davies, the book's designer.

1779

Stoneware dish
by Tatsuzo
Shimaoka, 1985.
Victoria and
Albert
Museum,
London.

CONTENTS

Tokyo street scene.

Motorbike,
Tokyo.

JAPANESE ARTS AND THE WEST

It is virtually impossible for an outsider to see another culture as it sees itself. After over a century of renewed contact with Japan, we recognise the products of an apparently Westernised economic superpower, but also the features of a culture firmly rooted in tradition.

The West has responded vividly to its glimpses of Japanese culture: artists from Degas to David

worlds, as do film-makers and composers. Toru Takemitsu, for example, writes music with titles reminiscent of Japanese paintings and poetry, but has also used the full forces of a modern symphony orchestra to create a film score, for *Ran* by Akira Kurosawa, who requested something 'like Mahler, but even more so', and wasn't disappointed.

So it may sometimes seem that fusion has taken place between Japanese and Western culture, when we see photos of Japanese Elvis Presley fans or the Tokyo Stock Exchange, a Japanese soprano as Madam Butterfly in Puccini's opera, the pianist Mitsuko Uchida playing Mozart or Seiji Ozawa conducting

Elvis Presley fans in Tokyo. Modern Japan has imported much of Western culture, from hamburgers and hairstyles to baseball, ballet and rock music.

Hockney, the composer Benjamin Britten, the potter Bernard Leach and the architect Frank Lloyd Wright have all been influenced by Japan. Japanese artists have in turn responded to the very different traditions of the West: Umehara Ryuzaburo (1888-1986), for example, studied with Renoir in 1910 and later became a professor in Tokyo. His Fauve-style painting of Mount Fuji recently sold for 1.4 million dollars at auction in New York.

Japanese fashion designers, often trained in Paris, straddle both

an American orchestra. But how much of a 'global village' do we really live in? The Japanese arts shown in this book are not picturesque survivals, but living arts central to a thriving and remarkably different culture from our own.

THE ROOTS OF JAPANESE CULTURE

The early pre-Buddhist religion of Japan is known today as Shinto, 'the way of the gods'. Japanese emperors were believed to descend from the Shinto sun goddess, and great heroes like the 16th- and 17th-century shoguns Hideyoshi and Ieyasu were also venerated in Shintoism, along with gods of war, fire, thunder and even rice, the staple food of Japan throughout its history. High mountains, tall and ancient trees and rivers are believed to house the gods and to have great spiritual strength; they have been worshipped since Japanese prehistory. Today Shinto rituals survive, for example, as part of Sumo wrestling and in many festivals.

Many important elements in Japanese culture originated in China but have been transformed: this is as true of religion as of food or architecture, the Tea Ceremony, ceramics, calligraphy and gardens. Chinese learning and writing took root in Japan from the early AD 400s, and the first permanent capital city, Nara, was modelled on the capital of T'ang China. Buddhism, which had originated in India centuries before, was introduced from China in 522 and became the official religion of Japan. In Japan, Buddhism in its many forms has managed to coexist with Shintoism, unlike with other religions in China. Japanese Buddhism has continually renewed itself, often with a Chinese stimulus. From the 12th century the Amida Buddha became the most attractive of intermediaries, inviting the faithful to his Western Paradise, which was often recreated symbolically on earth in temple gardens. His sensitive understanding of our sufferings on earth is well expressed in elegant medieval Japanese sculpture.

Medieval Japan, like medieval Europe, was a turbulent world dominated by warriors, or samurai (see pp.35-7). Japanese warlords, like the more cultivated Gothic kings, also patronised the arts and even wrote poetry. Until the 1860s the shogun was the real military ruler of Japan, while the emperors were mere figureheads. A 12th-century shogun like Yoritomo Minamoto, founder of the Kamakura shogunate, wished to be remembered as an administrator and builder of institutions, and as the founder of a dynasty rather than a hero in armour; and that is how we see him in his portrait (p.6), a formula still found in portraits of the 1600s.

In the late 13th century Japan survived two attempts at invasion by the armies of Kublai Khan, Mongol emperor of China. But only just: in 1281 the 'divine winds' (*kamikaze*) intervened and smashed the Chinese fleet to pieces. Chastened by their narrow escape, the samurai looked for new sources of spiritual and physical strength and often found them in Zen Buddhism. Zen first came to Japan from China in the 7th century and then more significantly in the late 12th century. It emphasised the individual's own ability to achieve salvation and renewal through meditation, which might take place in a monastery but might also be a

Above Painted and lacquered wood sculpture, probably depicting the retired head of a merchant family who has taken Buddhist priest's vows. An image of meditation and serenity. About 1700.

Right A 7th-century wooden image in the Chuguji convent, Nara, of the Bodhisattva Miroku contemplating the salvation of mankind. An early piece of Buddhist sculpture in Japan, it is strongly influenced by Chinese and Korean art.

part of daily life, such as contemplating a garden, or through calligraphy, poetry, the Tea Ceremony or martial arts. This philosophy has continued to be one of the essential strengths of the Japanese character in the late 20th century. Through Buddhism many Japanese have become reconciled to the incompleteness and imperfections of nature and life and to value them.

By the early 1600s Japan was trading with several foreign countries. The most powerful samurai, the *daimyo* (the equivalent of English barons) encouraged economic developments from their provincial castles, and the population grew. By 1600, for example, Kyoto, the capital city, which had been ruined by war in the 15th century, had revived with a population of perhaps a million people and was one of the largest cities in the world. The decisive battle of Sekigahara in 1600 established the rule of one family - the Tokugawa - as shoguns for the next 250 years, but for most of this time Japan was largely cut off from the outside world and its culture developed in isolation.

Yoritomo Minamoto (1147-99), first shogun at Kamakura. This hanging scroll painted on silk is an early 14th-century copy of a 12th-century portrait.

WESTERNERS IN JAPAN

Cultural contact between Japan and the West is a relatively modern phenomenon and has been neither continuous nor one-way. It began with the era of European exploration after the Renaissance, driven partly by the search for new sea routes to the East for the spice trade. In 1542 three Portuguese traders were blown off course and landed in Japan. Soon many other merchants as well as Catholic missionaries arrived.

18th-century wooden *netsuke* of a Dutchman holding a cockerel. He is making a gesture of derision by pulling down his eyelid with a finger. The Japanese were clearly impressed by the amount of meat Europeans ate (the Japanese didn't eat meat) and by their large noses.

The Portuguese brought Christianity, muskets and cannon, tobacco and playing cards, woollen clothes and Western cooking. Western innovations, whether metal armour or copper processing, were described as *Namban*, 'Southern Barbarian'. Europeans brought back from Japan lacquer furniture, gold, copper, silver, porcelain, rice, soy sauce, umbrellas and kimonos. Japanese paper was highly prized: Rembrandt was using it for etchings by the 1640s.

When in 1601 the shogun Ieyasu established his family as rulers of Japan, he made Edo (now Tokyo) his capital; the emperors continued to live at Kyoto until 1867, when they were restored to power and moved to Tokyo (which means 'the eastern capital'). Because of the bitter rivalry between the Europeans in Japan and the zeal of the missionaries, the shogun barred nearly all foreigners, so for much of this period Japan was cut off from the outside world. From 1639 Chinese and Dutch merchants were the only foreigners allowed into the country. The Japanese were forbidden to travel abroad or to build ocean-going ships.

Japan's isolation was ended by force. In July 1853 Commodore Matthew Perry arrived on the coast near Edo with four American battleships, causing great panic. He demanded that America be allowed to trade with Japan. Soon Britain, Russia, France, Germany and Holland were also allowed to trade in five Japanese ports. Following initial curiosity and often amusement, there was a great deal of hostility to these 'hairy barbarians'.

Following civil war in 1867-8, the Imperial forces established the emperor Meiji as the real ruler of Japan in place of the shogun. Rapid change followed: steam trains and

A Portuguese trumpeter in painted wood, c.1600. Purely decorative woodcarvings like this are not a feature of traditional Japanese art. The Japanese carver seems fascinated by European breeches and exposed legs, both of which he has exaggerated.

the telegraph, heavy industry such as shipbuilding and armaments, and Western clothes, food and ideas on education were adopted by the Japanese. In a popular rhyme of 1878, children counted the bounces of a ball while reciting ten desirable Western objects: gas lamps, steam engines, horse carriages, cameras, telegrams, lightning conductors, newspapers, schools, letter-post and steam boats.

In the 9th century a popular slogan had proposed 'Chinese knowledge, Japanese spirit'. In the 19th century the slogan was to become 'Western science, Eastern ethics'. By 1889 there was a constitution and a form of Parliament, but many Japanese, like the leading liberal reformer Fukuzawa Yukichi (1835-1901), were worried that Japan was becoming too Westernised:

'People say that foreigners are righteous, reasonable and deeply charitable ... but the evidence of my own eyes tells me that it is rubbish ... A country should not fear to defend its freedom against interference, even though the whole world is hostile.' (Barr 1970, p.79.)

When Japan proved its ability to do just that by defeating Russia in 1905, the world was astonished. Japan had become the first modern power in Asia to defeat a Western nation.

'An Account of the Opening of the Port of Yokohama' (1880), showing foreign sailors drunk in the streets. In the same book there are also illustrations of the Western world, some of them imaginary.

JAPONISME: WESTERN ARTISTS AND JAPANESE PRINTS

'Even the most vulgar Japanese sheets [of woodblock prints] coloured in flat tones are as admirable as Rubens and Veronese.' (Vincent van Gogh, *Letters*.)

Just as Picasso after 1900 found in non-European art a liberation from Western traditions of depicting the human figure, so his predecessors in Paris from the 1860s were inspired by the Japanese print. For Camille Pissarro (1831-1903), 'these Japanese confirm my belief in our vision'; to others, Japanese artists like Hokusai were 'the first and most perfect of the Impressionists'.

In 1856, just as Japan was first

Baudelaire. Soon Japanese prints were all the rage in Paris. The first major painter to respond was Edouard Manet (1832-83). In his portrait of Emile Zola (1868, Louvre, Paris), a fellow enthusiast for Japanese art, Manet portrays the novelist against a Japanese screen.

Zola compared the simplified style of Manet's paintings with Japanese prints, with 'their strange elegance and splendid colour patches'. Japanese printmakers used flat blocks of colour, without shading, and concentrated on line rather than volume. This was what attracted 19th-century artists reacting against Romanticism, who were seeking a cleaner, clearer palette of colours, a

Edouard Manet: *The Races*. Lithograph, late 1860s. Manet here uses the exaggerated vanishing point derived from European art by Japanese printmakers (see the print on the left and that on p.12).

opening to the West, a French printmaker, Félix Bracquemond, found some Japanese prints and showed them to his friends, including the poet Charles

new kind of composition and new subjects, notably 'modern life'. Manet, Edgar Degas (1834-1917) and Henri de Toulouse-Lautrec (1864-1901) capture the excitement of the horse races from unusual angles and with an immediacy both learnt from the Japanese print. At the circus, the ballet or the café, Degas and Lautrec look up at the tightrope or diagonally across the orchestra pit to the stage. Degas also painted subjects like women washing themselves, often seen from behind or from the side, as in the prints of Utamaro.

Degas and the Japanese print were the two strongest influences on

Christopher Dresser: Ceramic tile for Minton, *c.*1880, showing the strong influence of Japanese motifs.

Edgar Degas: *Leaving the Bath.* Pencil drawing over a lithograph, 1891. The subject of a woman bathing, combing her hair or with her maid is familiar from Japanese prints, which often show her from behind because the back and the nape of the neck were thought to be her most expressive features.

Lautrec, who is best known for his bold colour lithograph posters. He captures, for example, the essence of Loie Fuller's high-kicking dance act at the Folies-Bergère (1893) in a swirl of calligraphic lines, the stage spotlights suggested by gold or silver powder (another Japanese idea). It is like a flash photograph taken from the orchestra pit, and indeed late 19th-century photographers were also influenced by Japanese prints, especially by the cropping at the edges.

By the end of his short life Lautrec had gone much further than any of his contemporaries in depicting the Parisian equivalent of the 'red light

Edouard Manet: *Raven's head, pekinese dog and netsuke cutters' signatures.* Lithograph, 1875. An extraordinary sheet linked to Manet's illustrations for Edgar Allen Poe's poem 'The Raven', translated into French by Stéphane Mallarmé. In portraying the raven and the dog (brought back from Japan) Manet uses the swift, spontaneous brushstrokes typical of a Japanese woodcut.

Henri de Toulouse-Lautrec: *Le Divan Japonais*. Lithograph poster, 1893. Literally 'the Japanese settee', this was a Paris café music-hall hung with silks and fans; the waitresses wore kimonos. The influence of Japanese prints can be seen in the highly compressed composition: we look across the profile of Jane Avril and over the orchestra pit to the cropped figure of the singer. Lautrec arranges the colour in flat masses, without shading or modelling. He used a Japanese inkstone and brushes, adapting the methods of woodblock prints to colour lithography.

district' of Edo that was seen in so many Japanese prints. He lived in a brothel and showed its employees as they were, waiting for customers, bored, no longer beautiful.

With his brother Theo, Vincent van Gogh (1853-90) collected over 400 Japanese prints, and he copied landscapes by Hiroshige for their composition and unusual viewpoint, rather like that of a low-flying bird. In his *Portrait of Père Tanguy* (1887, Musée Rodin, Paris), the old man sits in front of a wall plastered with Japanese prints.

In 1876 the American artist James McNeill Whistler (1834-1903) had designed a Japanese-style interior, the Peacock Room (now in the Freer Gallery, Washington), for a house in London that also contained his painting *The Princess from the Land of Porcelain* (1863-4). The West had long been importing Japanese porcelain as well as lacquer, but now Westerners began to understand the whole Japanese approach to design, which did not distinguish between art and craft and which permeated everything from clothes to interiors.

Japanese arts became familiar in the West through publications and major exhibitions attracting key figures like William Morris and Sir Arthur Lasenby Liberty, founder of the famous London shop which then specialised in oriental arts. Similarly, L.C. Tiffany popularised Japanese art in the USA. Among those inspired by Japanese arts, furniture and interiors were Charles Rennie Mackintosh (1868-1928) and E.W. Godwin (1833-86), British pioneers of modern design, and French designers of glass and jewellery like Emile Gallé (1846-1904) and René Lalique (1860-1945). Alongside serious researchers like the designer Christopher Dresser (1834-1904), who visited Japan in 1876-7, there were dilettante collectors of erotic prints like Aubrey Beardsley (1872-98) and the other pallid aesthetes lampooned by Gilbert and Sullivan in *Patience* (1882) and *The Mikado* (1884).

Japanese arts strongly influenced the flowing line of Art Nouveau, as in the posters of the Czech artist Alphonse Mucha (1869-1939). The Viennese artists Gustav Klimt (1862-1918) and Egon Schiele (1890-1918) were avid collectors of Japanese prints.

As Europeans learned more about Japan and Japanese art, so Japonisme faded, and by the 1920s was virtually dead. No longer cut off from Europe, Japan was itself responding to the latest Western styles.

WOODBLOCK PRINTS

Woodblock prints and illustrated books are some of the most familiar and accessible of Japanese arts for us in the West. Woodblock printing is still a living art today: a British artist like Rebecca Salter, for example (see pp.14-15), has been trained in the traditional techniques by a Japanese master.

Like many other features of Japanese culture, printing came from China. It was controlled by the Buddhists and available only to priests and the aristocracy until the Edo period (1603-1867). The new urban culture of Kyoto, Osaka and Edo created a leisured wealthy class who wanted pictures of their world to be easily available. Soon there were hundreds of printing houses. Instead of aristocratic paintings, there were hand-coloured printed books, and then, to meet the enormous demand by the end of the 18th century, coloured prints made using woodblocks.

A finished print was the result of collaboration between publisher, artist, block-cutter and printer. Using a different block for each colour was obviously labour-intensive and therefore slow and expensive. They solved the problem of precise registration (how to fix the sheet onto the block so that the coloured shapes printed exactly where intended). Colours were not mixed to produce shades as in Western art, but used as separate and uniform blocks, strengthened or darkened by adjusting the amount of water or white pigment.

Woodblock prints might illustrate a great epic of Japanese literature, such as *The Tale of Genji*, or be part of a new collaboration between novelist and artist: between 1807 and 1811, for example, Hokusai illustrated a 30-volume serial novel by the writer Bakin. The prints might depict plants, insects or animals (see pp.18-19). They might illustrate manuals and accounts of different crafts, like the print of the Arita pottery on page 32. During this period, foreign travel was forbidden, and there was a growth of interest in the regions of Japan itself. For example, the 350-mile coastal road from Edo to Kyoto, the Tokaido, was depicted in a famous series of prints by Hiroshige.

The word *Ukiyoe* was originally used by Buddhists to mean this 'fleeting world', the short life of people on earth. In the Edo period it came to mean 'floating world' or having as good a time as possible because life is short. Ukiyoe prints therefore show the Japanese at play, for instance at the theatre (p.48) and

Katsushika Hokusai (1760-1849): *Portrait of himself as a fisherman watching the moon, c.1835.* Hokusai, 'the man mad about drawing', was well known as an eccentric and was described on his tomb as 'renowned, original, sincere man'. His work represents the epitome of the Ukiyoe style, and includes some of the most famous of all Japanese prints.

in the so-called 'Green Houses' of the Yoshiwara district (above). We see people viewing waterfalls and cherry blossom, gathering spring flowers or catching fireflies (p.20), picnicking on the beach or the river, eating in a restaurant (p.60), and invariably modelling the very latest fashions (p.43). From about 1830 Prussian blue was added to a repertoire of colours that included yellow, purple, orange and red; sometimes metal or mineral dusts were added or lacquered effects created by mixing glue with black ink.

When Japan ceased to be cut off from the outside world in 1853, an enormous and often undiscriminating demand for Ukiyoe prints arose in the West. At the same time, Japanese artists were exposed to the whole range of

European art. The result was a confusion and drop in standards that lasted until about 1900. Twentieth-century printmakers, however, have been extraordinarily active. Examples of traditional subjects in woodblock by Koshiro Onchi and Hiroshi Yoshida appear on pages 17 and 53. Besides woodblock, contemporary Japanese printmakers have many Western techniques at their disposal. An excellent example of a contemporary silkscreen is the print of sumo wrestlers by Ay-o (p.38). Kaoru Saito's *Swallowtails* (p.43) is a combination of mezzotint and aquatint, while Maku Haki combines cement, mortar and woodblock in his simulation of a raku bowl (p.27).

Torii Kiyotada (active *c*.1720-50): *The Daimonjiya brothel, c.*1745-50. This hand-coloured print shows a particularly exaggerated use of European perspective (learned from Dutch engravings) to a 'vanishing point' at the far end. Male customers are relaxing in one of the 'Green Houses' of the Yoshiwara district of Edo: smoking, playing a board game and listening to music played by one of the accomplished courtesans.

Right Utagawa Kunisada, 1786-1864 (Toyokuni III): *A sudden summer shower*, 1848-52. As lightning flashes, everyone runs for cover: one elegant lady shuts the sliding screens and another dives under a mosquito net (in Japanese folklore lightning never strikes a mulberry field or a mosquito net). Showing people through the fine mesh of a mosquito net gave printmakers a chance to display their skill. This print is in three sheets.

Above Katsushika Hokusai: *The great wave off Kanagawa*, from 'The Thirty-Six Views of Fuji', *c.*1830. Hokusai here uses the newly available Prussian blue pigment. The use of perspective and shading show Western influence, but the composition and the claw-like wave ends are purely Japanese.

Woodblock Printing Step by Step

Rebecca Salter is a British artist who went to Japan in the 1970s, initially to study pottery in Kyoto but later switching to woodblock printing. Because only screen printing and lithography, and not woodblock printing, were taught as 'contemporary' techniques in art schools, she studied at summer schools and classes with the Japanese printmaker Akira Kurosaki (b.1937), who has taught in America and whose prints are in foreign collections, including the British Museum.

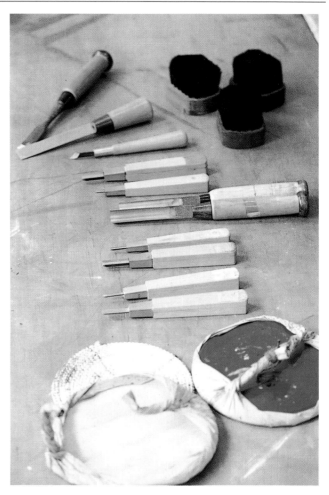

Rebecca uses 9 mm ply for her blocks, as cherry (the traditional Japanese material) is so expensive. She bought her cutting tools in Japan: all the blades were made by a former samurai sword maker.

After cutting the blocks (which may take a day or more) Rebecca wets them, adds glue and then inks them.

Rebecca carefully fits the paper into place: she uses machine-made paper imported from Japan. She then presses the paper down onto the block with a pad called a *baren*. This is a bamboo reed coil with laminated and lacquered covers, and may cost hundreds of pounds.

After she has printed each colour she peels the paper off the block and then inks up again in another colour. For an edition of 30-40 she would do all the sheets in one colour and then in the second colour, storing the sheets in damp paper until they were needed again.

One design can be printed in a variety of colour combinations.

Four Views of Mount Fuji

All mountains are sacred in Japan, according to Shintoism. Most sacred of all is Fuji, a volcano which has been dormant since 1707. At 3,766 metres, it is also the highest. Before modern development, Fuji was clearly visible from Tokyo, and obsessed many Edo artists, notably Hokusai.

Right Photograph of Fuji, seat of the Shinto gods.

Below Katsushika Hokusai: *A favourable breeze and clear weather, c.*1830. 'Red Fuji' is from Hokusai's 'Thirty-Six Views of Fuji', in which he established landscape as an important subject for printmakers. By wiping off some of the colour before printing the block, Hokusai has produced subtle shading effects. The grain of the cherrywood block is visible as lines on the mountain.

Left Katsushika Hokusai: *Fuji from the umbrella makers in Aoyama*, from 'One Hundred Views of Fuji', 1834-49. An illustration from the three volumes that were hugely influential in both Japan and the West. It is almost a case of 'spot the mountain' amid the wealth of wonderfully constructed detail.

Above Koshiro Onchi (1891-1955): *Mount Fuji in autumn*, from 'Fresh Praise of Fuji', 1946. A woodblock print like the others here but much more textured and with a strongly expressionist use of colour. Both Onchi and the poet Maeda whose work he is illustrating are here deliberately returning to the roots of Japanese culture, seeking spiritual strength after the turmoil of the Second World War.

'Living only for the moment, turning our full attention to the pleasures of the moon, the snow, the cherry blossoms and the maple leaves; singing songs, drinking wine, diverting ourselves in just floating, floating; refusing to be disheartened, like a gourd floating along the river current: this is what we call the floating world.' (Ryoi Asai, 'Ukiyo Monogatari', c.1661, translated by Richard Lane in *Images from the Floating World*, p.11.)

The Japanese attitude to the pleasures of nature is different from

Sato Suiseki (active c.1805-40): *A flock of birds*, from the artist's picture-album of 1820, which consists entirely of prints of flowers, birds and still life. A good example of the diagonal composition often seen in Japanese prints.

Matsumoto Hoji (active c.1785): *Frog*, from 'Picture-Album by Celebrated Artists', 1814.
'The ancient pond -
A frog jumps in,
The sound of water.'
Haiku by Matsuo Basho (1644-94).

that of the West: Shintoism, for example, teaches great respect for all living things; and the viewing of cherry blossoms, maple leaves, snow or flower arrangements are still popular and important occasions. The fascination with the natural world can be seen in the skilful depictions of plants and creatures on these pages, while the scenes of night and day on pages 20-21 show the technical brilliance of the greatest Japanese printmakers.

Ukiyoe and the Natural World

Above Hishikawa Moronobu (d.1694): *Bears and monkeys*, from the 'Complete Picture-Book of Animals', 1694. One of the great early pioneers of the Ukiyoe print here shows Japanese bears, with the white crescent on their fur.

Opposite Kitagawa Utamaro (1753-1806): *Grasshopper, Chinese bell-flower and pinks*, from 'Picture-Book of Selected Insects', 1788.

Night

Right Eishosai Choki (active late 1700s - early 1800s): *Catching fireflies, c.*1795. Against a summer night-time background of powdered black mica, the woman holds a firefly cage as the boy waits to catch them with his fan. The effects in this print are as rich and dramatic as any painter could hope to achieve.

Left Ando Hiroshige (1797-1858): *Seba, c.*1840. This is one of the prints from Hiroshige's famous series 'The Sixty-Nine Stations on the Kisokaido Road'. Hiroshige has created a magical and virtually imaginary moonlit landscape: if this is Seba, there should be mountains and a narrow river. The tension between trees and barge poles slanting in opposite directions gives a sense of movement to the two boats.

and Day

Left Eishosai Choki: *New Year sunrise, c.*1795. This important event in the calendar was best watched over the sea. Notice the stone basin for purification, with a ladle. The plant symbolises the New Year, and the woman is probably in her best clothes. A 14th-century court lady, Lady Nijo, remembers: 'As the mist rose among the spring bamboo heralding the dawn of the new year, the ladies of Go-Fukakusa's court, who had so eagerly awaited this morning, made their appearances in gorgeous costumes, each trying to surpass the others in beauty.'

Right Kitagawa Utamaro: *Drawing water for breakfast,* 1795-1800. Two servant girls are starting work by drawing water from the well. Utamaro uses a crowded image to create a feeling of frantic activity (perhaps they've overslept?) as they fix their hair.

CALLIGRAPHY

18th-century black lacquer writing box with gold and silver decoration, containing brush, knife-holders, ink stick, inkstone and water-dropper.

Calligraphy (*shodo*, 'the way of writing') came to Japan from China with Buddhism. Unlike Western writing, it uses characters which may each consist of as many as twenty strokes, written in columns from right to left across the page (possibly derived from early Chinese writing on bamboo strips). The Far Eastern calligrapher kneels on the floor and uses what the Chinese call the 'Four Treasures': brushes of rabbit, deer and goat hairs bound with silk thread in a bamboo tube and held vertically between thumb and index finger; a block of solid ink made of lamp black and glue; an inkstone on which to grind and wet the ink afresh each time it is needed, to the required shade; and a wide range of papers that may be coloured, decorated with mica paste or gold and silver motifs, perhaps with carefully torn edges or arranged in overlapping sheets.

In China and Japan calligraphy has for centuries been an important art, respected along with painting and poetry as the mark of a cultured person, whose character is revealed by the style and quality of his or her writing.

The characteristically terse style of Japanese poetry, found also in China, was ideally suited to calligraphy because the whole poem could be visualised as a picture: 'The wild goose has flown,/the seedling rice is dry./Gone is the blossom the water once reflected.' Sometimes the characters might be arranged on a painted screen to suggest reeds or birds.

For many centuries Japanese men wrote in Chinese while women used a much smaller number of Japanese characters in their own script and calligraphic style, 'women's hand'. The disciplined spontaneity of Zen paintings, with a few careful brushstrokes in varying shades of black ink, controlled by the pressure of the brush, originates in the free style of calligraphy developed by court ladies from the Heian period (794-1185) onwards.

The many styles and schools of calligraphy have such evocative names as 'dripping dew', 'tadpole', 'waves breaking', 'swimming goose' and 'falling leek'. 'Wild grass' supposedly derives from a Chinese

Harada Kampo (b.1911), one of Japan's leading calligraphers: 'When I take up an ink stick and rub it down on an inkstone, serenity and peace flow from my heart.'

monk who, while drunk, slapped huge characters onto pots and clothes as well as paper, and even soaked his hair in ink and wrote with it.

Hanging scrolls of calligraphy or paintings edged in gold brocade or silk were selected for contemplation and discussion during the Tea Ceremony (pp.28-9). Kobori Enshu (1579-1647) was a leading Edo tea master, calligrapher and landscape gardener. Other leading Edo calligraphers like Honami Koetsu (1558-1637) would also be connoisseurs of swords, painting, lacquer and pottery, and sought to develop a distinctly Japanese calligraphic style.

Today the Japanese script is an amalgam of Chinese and Japanese, with the 15,000 characters (originally selected from the 40,000 Chinese) reduced to 1,956. Even so, it still takes Japanese schoolchildren on average two years longer than European children to learn to read and write. A reforming Japanese education minister in the 1880s recommended abandoning the traditional system of writing because he thought it was holding Japan back technologically, but this does not in fact appear to have happened. Calligraphy remains an important link between Japan old and new, and ancient examples are very highly prized and expensive.

Below Kitagawa Utamaro (1753-1806): *The hour of the dog,* from 'The Twelve Hours of the Green Houses'. A courtesan is writing to her lover on a long roll of handmade paper.

Left Takuan Soko (1573-1643): *Like moving clouds and running water.* Hanging scroll, 1636. Soko was abbot of the Zen Buddhist monastery of Daitokuji in Kyoto, which has a famous Zen garden and was closely linked to the Urasenke tea masters. Calligraphy like this might hang in a tea house. Lent to the British Museum by the Urasenke Tea Foundation, Kyoto.

ORIGAMI

The term origami comes from the Japanese characters for the verb *oru,* to fold, and the noun *kami,* paper. Before the mid-19th century it was known by other terms such as *orikata* and *orisue.*

The tradition of paper folding in Japan has its roots in Shinto. The symbolic representation of a deity

Above Traditional origami forms made by children at the Bethnal Green Museum of Childhood, London.

Below Origami models arranged as a pattern for wooden panels, from *Ramma zushiki,* a woodcut book illustrated by Shumboku, 1734.

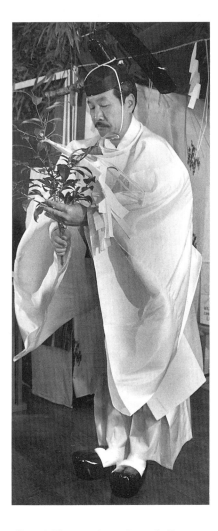

Above A Shinto priest using *gohei* in a purification ritual at the ground-breaking ceremony *(kikoshiki)* for the new Japanese galleries at the British Museum in 1987.

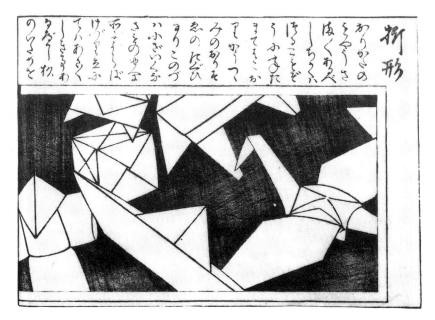

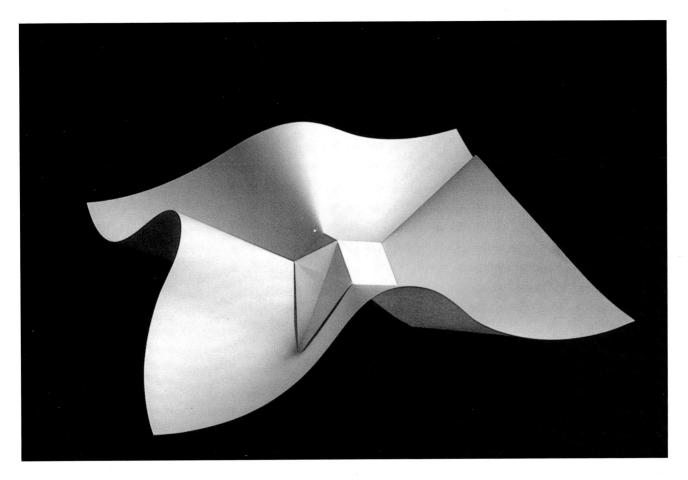

An abstract paper form by contemporary British paper-folder Paul Jackson, *c*.1984.

(*katashiro*) was cut from paper made especially for the Shinto shrine. Forms of *katashiro* can still be found today, particularly in the paper dolls displayed annually in homes at the Doll Festival in March and in the form known as *gohei* or *o-shide* used in Shinto purification rituals. Other traditional forms of origami include the folded butterfly attached to *sake* bottles at a Japanese wedding, and *noshi*, an elongated, open-ended hexagonal shape with strings which is attached to gifts.

Various forms of origami were passed on from parent to child, and by the Edo period, when more popular techniques had been developed, such was the interest in origami that several books were published giving instructions on folding certain forms. In the later 19th century origami was introduced into primary schools, where traditional forms were taught as an enjoyable way of learning coordination and understanding the relationship between a plane and a solid form.

One form which deserves special mention is the crane, a bird which in Japan symbolises long life and good fortune. Since the Second World War it has also been a symbol of peace. A young girl, Sadako Sasaki, dying of radiation sickness after the atomic bomb explosion at Hiroshima, hoped to fold 1,000 cranes as a prayer for universal peace but completed only 644 before she died. In 1958 a monument was erected to her in Hiroshima Park. Thousands of paper cranes were attached to it, and many are still sent there today.

Today's creative origami has been influenced and stimulated by the work of Akira Yoshizawa (b.1911), a Japanese artist who uses paper to construct abstract and representational art-forms. Although there are indigenous forms of paper folding in the West, it was Yoshizawa's exhibition in Amsterdam in 1955 that sparked off the upsurge of interest in origami in the West today.

As well as the traditional forms which are still taught, many thousands of other forms are now practised. Some contemporary paper folders, such as the Englishman Paul Jackson, create subtle forms by the gentle, soft folding of paper where the use of light and shade are just as important to the finished form as the folding itself.

POTTERY

Raku

Peter Hayes demonstrating raku at the Crafts Study Centre, Bath, in 1987.

Pottery first developed in Japan 8,000 to 9,000 years ago and achieved technical precision very early, as it did in China and Korea, whose ceramics have strongly influenced many Japanese potters right up to the present day. One of the most influential Japanese developments has been *raku*. The word 'ranges in meaning from ease, comfort or enjoyment, to happiness'. It was a compliment awarded to the great potter Tanaka Chojiro (1516-92) in honour of his tea bowls by the ruler of Japan, Toyotomi Hideyoshi (1536-98). Chojiro's successors in Kyoto have been called 'Raku' ever since. Raku XV succeeded to his title in 1980: his work is greatly admired and very expensive.

The essence of a raku pot is that it should appear 'natural' rather than perfect in shape or glaze. Because the clay for raku may include ground-up flints and sand, the surface of the pot will never be smooth like porcelain. The results of the process are often unpredictable, which is one of its attractions for contemporary potters, as is its often crazed or crackled glaze. Raku is hand-built rather than thrown, and its soft surface allows for a unique combination of thumb impressions and other marks.

Tea bowls are cupped in the hand during the Tea Ceremony, and with repeated use this produces the ceramic equivalent of a patina on bronze. As they have no handles, the bowls are made so that they are not too hot to hold when full of tea.

The raku glaze has a high proportion of lead (up to 70%) and is generally dark; after perhaps 15 minutes in the kiln the glaze melts

Left A 17th-century water jar for the Tea Ceremony, with a dark brown glaze with lighter flecks where it has failed in the firing.

Below A 17th- or 18th-century raku tea bowl with black and brown glaze.

and then hardens as it cools rapidly outside. Judging the right moment to take the pot out of the kiln requires great skill. Raku is fired at the low temperature of about 750° C (roughly the heat at the heart of a bonfire), compared with 1350° C for oriental porcelain, 1220° C for salt-glazed stoneware, or 900-1100° C for lead-glazed slipware.

Today 'raku' is also used quite loosely to describe contemporary work by some Japanese and some Western potters such as Hal Riegger (author of a book on raku). These potters may perhaps smother a piece in sawdust or drown it in sump oil outside the kiln to produce dramatic effects quite unlike the traditionally calm raku tea bowl.

Below Haku Maki (b.1924): *Collection 85-10*, 1985. A pupil of the great mid-20th-century printmaker Koshiro Onchi (see p.17), Maki here combines the traditional woodblock print, seal and signature in characters with a modern mixed-media simulation of a raku bowl using cement and mortar.

The Way of Tea

Chojiro's raku tea bowls were commissioned by the great tea master and Zen priest Sen-no-Rikyu (1521-91). He developed the ceremony of preparing, offering and drinking tea into a ritual of meditation, which is an essential part of Zen Buddhism. *Chado* means 'way of tea' and *cha-no-yu* 'hot water for tea', but there is far more to it than that. Today, like a Zen garden, the Tea Ceremony offers a little peace in the middle of a hectic urban life. A full four-hour ceremony begins with a light meal of soups, rice, fish, vegetables and cake, followed by a pause for digestion and meditation, a thick tea and then a foaming thinner tea. The one-hour ceremony consists of the latter on its own. Normally not more than five people are involved, and they move quietly, slowly and gracefully from the waiting room (often an open pavilion in a garden) to the tea house.

A tea house has walls of paper or mud and a ceiling of rush or bamboo: its size is measured in lengths of *tatami* matting. Everything in the tiny, simple tea house and garden must be harmonious, scrupulously clean and properly arranged, but not ostentatious. The tea bowls must be pleasing to touch but not distracting in design, and therefore not brightly

Above An unusually early example of European collecting of Japanese tea ware: this tea bowl with white brushed decoration under a black-brown glaze was made *c.*1690 at Utsusugawa and bought in 1753 by Sir Hans Sloane, whose collections formed the nucleus of the British Museum.

Below A portable set of tea utensils, including tea bowl, caddy, bamboo whisk and paper-napkin holder. 17th-18th centuries.

Learning the art of the Tea Ceremony. Many Westerners have trained to become masters of the art.

or busily decorated. Their colour should contrast attractively with the powdered green tea (considered medicinal) and with the white froth on top of the tea once it has been whipped up with a bamboo whisk. The tea master will also need special food dishes, rests for the kettle lid and ladle, tea caddies, slop basins, and vases that may hold one flower appropriate for the time of year or the mood of the occasion. These pots, in particular the raku bowls, contrast with other Japanese ceramics, including those made for export and the fine porcelain tea bowls or teapots made in China and copied in the West.

The ceremony ends with the guest of honour asking to look more closely at the pots and utensils, and starting a conversation about them. As a historian of ceramics has said, 'nowhere, perhaps, has the pursuit of aesthetic sensibility become more generally ingrained in a nation than in Japan' (Ayers, p.65). In the 'way of tea' the Japanese aim for a feeling of *wabi* - profound, peaceful, and 'finding satisfaction in poverty'.

The tea house at Jo-an, built in 1618 by a disciple of the great tea master Sen-no-Rikyu.

Leach and Hamada

Japanese ceramics have had a remarkable and far-reaching impact on potters all over the world. This is particularly due to the influence of the English potter Bernard Leach (1887-1979), who spent the years 1909-20 in Japan and returned there several times.

Leach was born in China, then grew up in England. Having had 'the two extremes of culture to draw

to the East to teach or to criticise ... few people come over here to learn from our side and still fewer are the foreigners who realise that we learn more from those who learn from us ... [Leach] plunged into his new life, of receiving ... so it is not surprising that his influence on us has been so great, and that there has been between him and us a community and understanding such as has

and factories. But Leach was disenchanted with the industrialised production of ceramics, which he considered 'inhuman'. He sought a reappraisal of traditional pottery, in both Europe and Japan, for its simplicity and lack of highly finished decoration. In the early years of the 20th century there was a reaction in all the arts against ornament and elaboration, for example in the work of painters like Picasso and the Cubists, architects like Le Corbusier and Loos (who thought that ornament was a criminal waste of human effort), composers like Schoenberg, who reacted against his own earlier lusher style, and designers like those of the Bauhaus in Germany between the wars. Leach cites parallels such as these in *A Potter's Book*, first published in 1940, which became a bestseller. He goes on to contrast the situation of the craftsman in the West, 'faced with a broken tradition' and 'with culture in rapid process of change', with what he had found in Japan: 'craftsmen of today need to recover a state where there is no strain between intuition, reason and action.'

'One day in 1911 [Leach remembers] I was invited to a sort of garden party at an artist friend's house in Tokyo ... brushes and saucers of colour were brought in and we were invited to write or paint upon [the pots] ... I was told that within an hour's time these pots would be glazed and afterwards fired in a little portable kiln, which a man was stoking with charcoal in the garden.'

Here Leach was witnessing the Japanese technique of raku for the first time. He was able to learn from a master: his teacher Kenzan VI was the sixth and last of a family of great potters. Leach also observed other survivors of a long tradition: for example, an illiterate old lady who painted as many as a thousand pots a day, and a man who could

Bernard Leach with Shoji Hamada in Japan in 1935.

upon', he said, 'it was this which caused me to return to Japan, where the synthesis of east and west has gone furthest'. A painter, printmaker and lecturer, Leach went to Japan to teach. While there, he became interested in pottery, having to learn the technique from scratch. His willingness to learn from the Japanese made a great impression on them:

'Most visitors from the West come

scarcely ever been reached before between ourselves and foreigners.' (Soyetsu Yanagi (1889-1961), founder of Mingei, the Japanese Folk Craft Movement, writing in 1940.)

Leach was not the first European potter to be interested in Japan: Japanese-style stoneware had been made in France from the 1890s and then in Northern Europe and America by both individual potters

in Japan. Leach's wife Janet, also a potter, remembers:

'[Hamada] was an avid museum visitor and never stopped looking at pots. He seemed to think pots at every minute. He constantly drew in his diary. He always said that seeing good crafts fed him. He said he "ate" them and needed them for his body more than rice.'

Like Leach, Hamada thought of the potter as an artist, living in harmony with his surroundings and his work:

'When I look at my pots coming out of the kiln, it is almost like a farmer pulling potatoes out of the ground.'

Left Bernard Leach: Cast stoneware bottle, 1969. Holburne Museum and Crafts Study Centre, Bath.

Below Shoji Hamada: Pottery tea bowl with iron brown brushstrokes under a dull celadon glaze.

hand-build a jar three feet high.

With the help of his Japanese pupil Shoji Hamada (1892-1978), Leach set up his pottery at St Ives in Cornwall in 1920. Here he introduced raku to the West; also the use of Japanese brushes for decoration that was calligraphic (using broad strokes rather than fine detailed painting), as well as Japanese glazes such as *tenmoku*, an iron glaze that is lustrous black with an effect of red rust on the thinner parts. Hamada researched traditional English pottery with Leach, and when he returned to Japan introduced salt glazes and forms such as the medieval English jug. In his search for authenticity of forms and truth to tradition he used a stick-operated manual wheel. From 1924 he worked in Mashiko, a traditional pottery centre north of Tokyo, and eventually became a 'living national treasure'

Porcelain

Porcelain was a Chinese invention of the 7th or 8th century AD, but not until the early 18th century did Europeans work out how to make it themselves. In the mid-17th century, Chinese porcelain was temporarily unavailable for export, due to political upheaval. Japanese porcelain was exported instead by the Dutch and was widely imitated in the 18th century at Meissen. In the 19th century it was especially popular in Victorian Britain and in North America. This ornate, colourful and often enamelled ware may also be used for the Tea Ceremony. The chief centre of porcelain making in Japan is Arita, seen in the print below.

Right A storage jar for leaf tea, dated 1805, decorated in the 'brocaded style' (imitating in enamels the brocade silk square that would be tied around the lid) with chrysanthemums and the family crests of the shoguns who ruled Japan.

Painting porcelain at Arita, from 'Noted Products from Land and Sea of Japan in Pictures' by Kangetsu, 1799. The hierarchy of jobs is clearly visible, with the robed master at the left decorating the pots. The 'assembly line' was developed to meet insatiable European demand via the Dutch trading posts in Japan.

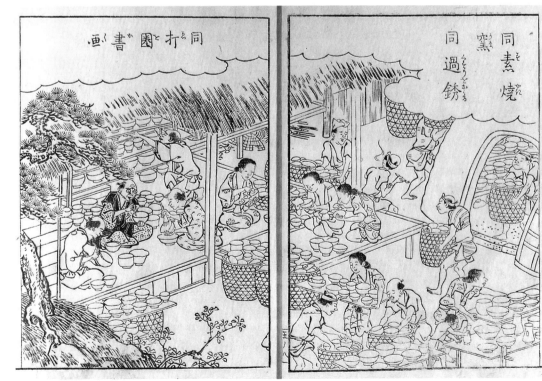

Contemporary Ceramics

stoneware dish with a diameter of 57 cm (illustrated on pp.2-3). He uses a combination of Eastern and Western techniques: underglaze iron painting and rope-impressed decoration are combined with the traditional European method of decorating the surface with a liquid clay mix called slip, which was popularised in Japan by another of Leach's Japanese friends and colleagues, Kenkichi Tomimoto.

A number of long dynasties of potters still have members at work in Japan today. Imaemon Imaizumi XIII was born in 1925 into a family of potters in Arita; his work uses traditional motifs such as the chrysanthemum and the

A recent survey of Japanese art and design remarks that 'in the world of contemporary art ceramics ... one might suggest that Japan is the leader in the field in terms of the large number of active potters, the high prices which they can command, and the wide variety of styles in which they work' (Earle, p.208). In the Victoria and Albert Museum collections it is possible to see something of this wide variety. Tatsuzo Shimaoka (b.1919) was Hamada's leading student and is regarded by many as Japan's foremost potter, but unlike Hamada or Leach he is not primarily concerned with producing functional pottery at relatively low prices. He makes 'art objects' for the collector or gallery: one of his pieces is a large

Above left Keiko Hasegawa at work in her Devon studio.

Above A raku water jar made by Keiko Hasegawa in the 1980s.

characteristic earlier Japanese technique of enamelling. Shinobu Kawase (b.1950) is the third generation of a family of potters working mainly in Chinese idioms, particularly following the style of the 12th- to 13th-century Song dynasty celadons long admired in Japan.

The British Museum has examples of work by Keiko Hasegawa (b.1941), whose family has worked in the cast-iron industry for over fourteen generations. She too has studied cast iron and bronze design, as well as ceramics: her raku pieces have a strongly metallic finish. Since 1977 she has lived in England, working with Bernard Leach's son Michael and now on her own in Devon. She uses a gas-fired kiln at 900-1000° C (higher than usual for raku) and has produced sculptural pieces as well as tea bowls, vases

and water jars. Like many contemporary Japanese artists, she exhibits throughout Europe as well as in Australia and Japan.

While anonymous folk potters in Japan maintain the traditions revived by Leach and Hamada and sell their work at Folk Art counters in department stores, 'avant garde' potters like Kazuo Yagi (1919-79) have been more experimental, and a major trend in recent ceramics has been towards pottery as sculpture. The Victoria and Albert Museum has examples of work by Shoji Kamoda (1933-83), who worked in Mashiko like Hamada and Shimaoka. He was especially interested in angular sculptural forms but often with a traditionally 'earthy' unpolished surface that was not glazed but had a 'wax-resist' decoration.

A set of raku boxes made by Hasegawa in the 1980s, showing the range of colours and metallic effects possible in her version of the technique.

SAMURAI AND SWORDS

Samurai means literally 'one who serves'. Initially in early medieval times the samurai were bodyguards for the Imperial court and leading nobles. But as the power of the emperor waned, the samurai attached themselves to great family clans which rampaged throughout the Japan of the 11th and 12th centuries. The leaders of the most powerful clans became shoguns from the end of the 12th century, and the leading samurai, the daimyo, established regional power-bases. Clan warfare erupted regularly until the shogun Ieyasu, following his victory at Sekigahara in 1600, sapped the power of the daimyo. Their families had to live permanently at court, and the warlords themselves likewise every other year, incurring the crippling expense of at least two households.

The medieval samurai followed a harsh code: 'our bodies shall repay our debts; our lives shall count as nothing where honour is at stake.' Splendid in a suit of iron armour made of scales lacquered and sewn together with coloured cords, bellowing his name, rank, ancestry and brave deeds, and identified by the small flag at his back, the samurai challenged his enemies in battle, claiming their heads as trophies. At first samurai were mounted archers, using bows taller than themselves; later archery was supplanted by swordsmanship. A samurai alone had two swords, and the sword became a great work of art and the subject of Shinto veneration.

Samurai were also expected to be cultivated people, able to appreciate poetry and art. A sword or saddle might be decorated with poetic symbols (waves, flowers, cobwebs), and a great commander might take part in the Tea Ceremony immediately after battle. Zen

Right Samurai armour: late 16th-century thick steel-plate bulletproof cuirass and sleeves; 17th-century helmet; the rest is 18th-19th century. Much of this armour is thus from the period after 1600, when armour for real warfare gave way to armour for display.

Buddhism was especially influential among samurai, stressing mental discipline but also spontaneity.

The wealth of a warlord was measured in *koku* - the amount of rice needed to feed a samurai for a year (Shogun Ieyasu was worth two and a half million *koku*). Samurai carried rice in thin bags strung round their necks, and cooked it in their iron helmets. The great castles where samurai were garrisoned when not fighting protected the adjoining rice fields and irrigation systems during civil war. Sixteenth-century visitors from Europe were enormously impressed by the grandeur and strength of the castles they saw, which were designed to withstand guns, introduced by the Portuguese. Part of the main castle of Edo survives today as the Imperial residence; Himeji castle is illustrated on page 53.

By the 16th century leading daimyo were encouraging the growth of market towns and trade. In the Edo period, after Ieyasu's reforms, they were still above the merchants in the social hierarchy, but frequently much poorer. There were no longer spoils of war, inflation cut into fixed incomes, and samurai had to learn to be officials or teach martial arts. Instead of supplying warriors and weapons, daimyo were now forced to contribute to the cost of rebuilding

castles and palaces and of work on roads, bridges and harbours. Armour became purely decorative. Modernisation continued: the medieval practice of *junshi* (ritual suicide) by a samurai on the death of his lord was banned, and attempts were made to help heavily indebted samurai. It was those daimyo who had come to terms with changed circumstances and reformed their finances who took the lead in

Left Assault on the Yashima fortress, from a 17th-century six-fold screen in ink, colours and gold-leaf on paper. This scene depicts a battle of the 1180s which brought Yoritomo Minamoto to power (see pp.5-6). Japanese literature has many accounts of epic battles: 'the great hero of the battle ... shot arrows from horseback like a god; undeterred by gleaming blades, he lunged ... he galloped like the wind and fought with a skill that was more than human.'

Below Model mounted samurai from the Bethnal Green Museum of Childhood, London. In the background Benkei confronts Yoshitune (who has leapt up onto a pillar) in a famous battle on a bridge, from a medieval epic.

overthrowing the shogun in the 1860s and restoring the emperor Meiji.

Following the restoration, daimyo were made peers but samurai fared less well; some continued to do similar jobs, as policemen, army officers or administrators. They had to give up their swords unless in the army or police, and their characteristic top-knot was banned; Western dress was to be worn on all official occasions.

In the 20th century, especially in wartime, some Japanese have referred back to the samurai by taking only swords into battle against machine-guns or making 'kamikaze' air-raids involving the death of the pilot as he deliberately crashes his plane, or even committing ritual suicide like the novelist Yukio Mishima in 1970. In reality the age of the samurai warrior was already over in the early 1600s, after their last great battle: today the romance lives on in films such as Kurosawa's *The Seven Samurai* and countless others, the cowboy westerns of the East. Samurai influences still persist: 'probably to a degree unmatched in any other culture, the Japanese have exalted such qualities as loyalty, faithfulness, devotion, dedication' (Herman Kahn).

Swords

Dagger blade, 30 cm long, carved with a motif of dragon and thunderbolt, c.1600.

Swordsmiths have always been regarded as the supreme craftsmen in Japan, as artists taking part in an almost religious ritual. The medieval sword was the soul of the samurai; even today a sword is given a name or a title, as in medieval Europe, and treated with great respect as a symbol of honour and loyalty.

The special characteristics of the Japanese sword - lethally sharp with a hard cutting edge and a softer interior to give some flexibility - have made it unequalled among the weapons of the world since the technology was first perfected over 1,000 years ago. A typical blade may be the result of many foldings of the steel, and contain over a million layers. The crucial moments in the process rely on the seasoned eye and intuition of the master:

'In the dark of night, with black curtains over the windows to keep out any stray moonlight, [the swordsmith Akihira] Miyairi supervises the heating of the forge, using cubes of charcoal prepared by the swordsmith himself. Adjusting the draught, raking the coals for the perfect temperature, moving the blade back and forth over the heat to distribute it correctly from the thin tip of the heavy ridge, Miyairi determines by colour the exact temperature of the steel and plunges the white hot blade into a wooden trough of water. This climactic quenching takes less than a minute. The cooled blade is then immediately inspected for flaws, since even a minute flaw renders the blade imperfect and acceptable only as a piece of steel.' (Birdsall, p.45.)

Ken Mishima, a leading Japanese sword-polisher, at work on one of the British Museum's collection of 200 blades.

Sword fittings, such as this *tsuba* (the sword guard between blade and hilt) became works of miniature sculpture, using brass, copper, gold inlay and alloys. They feature coiled dragons, flowers and birds, family crests and Buddhist guardian figures, as here.

SUMO AND MARTIAL ARTS

Western sports like baseball are increasingly popular in Japan, but the most popular of the traditional spectator sports is still sumo wrestling. Whereas the martial arts, which include judo, kendo and karate, have been strongly influenced by Buddhism (and have served in the past as practical training for samurai), sumo, which is not a martial art, originated with the earlier Shinto religion, perhaps 2,000 years ago. Sumo tournaments were held, along with dancing and drama, at Shinto shrines as part of

harvest thanksgivings from at least the 8th century AD. Today the referee at a sumo match is still dressed as a Shinto priest, and the canopy above the ring resembles a Shinto shrine, with four giant tassels symbolising the four seasons.

Sumo has been a professional sport since the mid-18th century and is watched by millions on TV in Japan and the West, but there is still a strong sense of ritual: before the match begins, each wrestler (*rikishi*) scatters salt to purify the ground, gargles 'power water' and makes

other ritual movements. There is a tense period of waiting for the first move, and the match may then be over in seconds. The essence of sumo is that one wrestler pushes the other out of the ring, or forces him to touch the ground other than with the soles of his feet. Even a fingertip on the ground may be enough to end the match. In order to develop weight and strength, the wrestlers combine hard training with hard eating: the heaviest sumo wrestler to date weighs over 200 kg (nearly 36 stone) and is a celebrity like a film star. A top-rank wrestler is known as a *yokozuna*, the name of the belt that is the only clothing permitted during the fight. Wrestlers may grapple by holding on to each other's belts; they may not pull their opponent's hair, gouge his eyes, kick or hit him.

Left A sumo match in Tokyo.

Above Sumo wrestling, 1984. Silkscreen print by Ay-o (b.1931), the adopted name of a Japanese painter and printmaker living in Tokyo. Heavily influenced by American art of the 1960s, he paints in acrylic and has made many other rainbow prints. This print is based on one by Utagawa Kunisada (Toyokuni III, 1786-1864).

Right An 18th-century ivory *netsuke* depicting two popular gods sumo wrestling. In Japanese mythology, it was as a result of another sumo contest that one of the gods gained control of the country.

Katsukawa Shun'ei (1762-1819): *The pre-match procession at a sumo tournament*, 1796. Sumo wrestlers are enormous, but not quite this big compared with their audience!

Martial arts

Combat schools in Japan date back to the 15th-century civil wars, and today you can still learn to use a samurai sword against an opponent dressed in samurai-style armour. But this is not some anachronistic war-game. Bushido, 'the way of the warrior', brings mental agility and mental peace. As one master of the martial arts has observed, 'without their philosophical content, the martial arts would be nothing more than the acquisition of animal-like brute strength.' In archery, kyudo, 'you may find your own character at the moment of shooting', to use a Zen phrase, with mind and body acting as one. In kendo ('the way of the sword'), using bamboo swords, action is so swift that it is impossible to prepare your move as in a more sedate sport: spontaneity goes hand in hand with *mushin*, the Zen concept of 'no mind'. Karate means 'empty hand', and developed originally on the island of Okinawa where weapons were banned from the 15th century. Like many of the martial arts, it developed in secrecy. Judo ('the way of gentleness') developed from Ju-Jitsu in the 1880s: it is the only martial art to be an Olympic sport, and has more than 8 million adherents in Japan today. Naginata-do ('the way of the halberd', a pikestaff weapon much used in the Middle Ages) has developed for women since the Edo period and has attracted 2 million Japanese members. New martial arts like aikido ('the way of divine harmony') have emerged since the 1930s and have spread worldwide, partly through American servicemen stationed in post-war Japan.

Above Kendo: an Englishman demonstrates a *men* or head-cut on his Japanese opponent, in an Oxford *dojo* (martial arts hall).

Left Prior to attack, participants in kendo perform rituals of respect.

CLOTHES

The *kimono*, which means 'the thing worn', is the Japanese garment traditionally worn by both men and women and still worn today on special occasions, for example by Japanese brides. Kimonos are loose garments, sometimes worn in layers, tied at the waist by a sash. Special devices called *netsuke* were invented to secure fans, bags, etc. to the waist, as kimonos have no pockets, buttons or zips. The design of the kimono inevitably focuses attention on the quality of the material and its decoration, rather than on the cut (except at the neck and sleeves) or indeed on the contours of the body inside, as is the case with generally tighter-fitting Western clothes.

The diversity of motifs on kimonos is quite extraordinary and unparalleled in Western textiles. The Victoria and Albert Museum in London has excellent examples of Japanese textiles, and the British Museum has recently collected several kimonos. To see a wider range of designs and to appreciate the flair and vitality of Japanese textiles, you might use Jeanne Allen's *Designer's Guide to Japanese Patterns* (1988-9). Here are bamboo leaves, ferns and grasses, cherry and apricot blossom and wisteria; spring willows, early summer swallows, carp swimming up waterfalls, waves and fans, butterflies, cranes (symbols of long life) and bats (popular with earlier samurai and then with Edo merchants). More abstract patterns are inspired by tortoise-shells, pots and baskets, or incorporate heraldic family crests. Sometimes lines from poems are included, or riddles or hidden messages. Fashionable people could choose their kimono patterns from black and white illustrated books, many of which still survive. To see the full effects of colour, we can turn to woodblock prints as well as museum collections.

In her *Confessions* (1307), Lady Nijo, a retired court lady, describes

Utagawa Kuniyoshi (1797-1861): *Notes on women's conduct - stretching fabrics, c.*1842. Servants are here washing a sash (*obi*) and hanging it out to dry. They are wearing wooden pattens (*geta*), here no doubt to prevent their hemlines from trailing in water and dirt. The way the *obi* is tied at the back denotes the age of the woman wearing it, and whether she is married (folded like a cushion) or single (in a large bow like a butterfly).

the care that was taken in combining colours, materials and linings:

'[At New Year] I recall wearing a layered gown shaded from light pink to dark red, with outer gowns of deep purple and light green and a red formal jacket. My undergown was a two-layered small-sleeved brocade patterned with plum blossoms and vines, and embroidered with bamboo fences and plum trees.'

Left Kitagawa Utamaro (1753-1806): *The outer robe*, c.1797. Utamaro is particularly famous for his depictions of 18th-century beauties and their clothes.

Below Kaoru Saito (b.1931): *Swallowtails*. Mezzotint/aquatint for the 'Red Illusion' series, 1983. One of Japan's most accomplished contemporary printmakers here combines the traditional Ukiyoe manner of depicting a beautiful woman and her clothes (showing the back of her neck, for example) with a fantasy quality reminiscent of the work of the Dutch artist M.C. Escher, especially in the way the swallowtails that seem to fly out of her robe turn from red to black. Her make-up is that of a court lady of centuries ago, but her earrings are of the 1980s.

Below A late 17th-century Kakiemon porcelain figure of a young man wearing a kimono. Men wear narrower sashes than women and do not tie them decoratively at the back.

A 20th-century kimono with a contrasting red lining.

A 19th-century green silk kimono with roundels of flowers and leaves embroidered in satin-stitch. The gold family crest can be seen on the shoulders. Victoria and Albert Museum, London.

A silk summer kimono, late Edo period, 19th century. This kimono has been dyed in indigo with patterns of bamboo and cranes reserved in white by wax-resist. These white areas were then embellished with coloured embroidery and hand-painted lines in black.

A 20th-century kimono with a stylised design using traditional motifs such as the samurai helmet.

Contemporary Fashion

Kimonos are no longer normal wear in Japan as they were even in the 1930s. Major Japanese fashion designers have trained in Paris, and are now well known internationally. Kenzo Takada was one of the first, with the 'Jap' label. In the 1970s he combined garish Western colours from the era of Pop Art with Japanese materials such as silks and natural cotton and the looser cut of the traditional kimono. He designs practical clothes for the working

woman - not too tight, stylish but not outrageous, and not at Paris prices.

Undoubtedly the most celebrated contemporary Japanese fashion designer is Issey Miyake. Miyake worked for Laroche and Givenchy in Paris in the 1960s, and shared in the anti-establishment feeling of the 1968 student riots. He reacted against

Left Designs by Issey Miyake being modelled at a Paris fashion show in 1989.

Right Clothes as origami? Miyake's oiled-paper raincoats (1984) show the sculptural quality of his more recent clothes and the way he uses and transforms traditions: 'I like to work in the spirit of the kimono. Between the body and the fabric there exists only an approximate contact' (Sparke, p.116).

the formality of highly tailored *haute couture*, and has become known for his loosely draped effects, often using several layers of natural fabrics. His mainstream clothes are designed as 'tools for living', but in his more experimental work he has created clothes as sculpture, notably in his exhibition 'Body Works' (1983), seen in the USA and England as well as in Japan.

Surprisingly, the Comme des Garçons chain of clothes and boutiques is Japanese, founded by Rei Kawakubo. She is traditional in her use of natural dyes, including calligrapher's ink, and in the way her designs are deliberately imperfect, like raku pots which emerge unpredictably from a kiln. What began as a reaction to the inhibiting effect of Western *haute couture* by a woman without formal fashion training has, like Miyake's work, turned into a new orthodoxy of anti-fashion.

THEATRE

The oldest surviving form of theatre in Japan is No, which dates back to the Middle Ages. It is very formal and slow-moving, with hypnotic dancing to drums and flute. Masks play a very important part, as does stylised gesture: a touch of the sleeve suggests happiness in love, a raised right hand can mean weeping. No, which unlike the more popular Kabuki theatre was associated with the court, has enjoyed a revival in the 20th century. The famous Japanese writer Yukio Mishima adapted several No plays for Western performance, and the British composer Benjamin Britten (1913-76) combined Japanese No drama and music with the medieval British mystery play to create his 'Parables for Church Performance', including *Curlew River* and *The Burning Fiery Furnace* (see p.59).

Kabuki theatre began in the early 17th century as a reaction to the aristocratic No theatre: the word means 'frolicking'. The first performances were entirely by women, but by 1629 this was thought to be scandalous and actresses were forbidden, as were boy actors, so adult male actors had to develop the ability to impersonate women. We can capture the spirit of Kabuki from 18th- and 19th-century prints and now have the chance in the West to see live performances by some of Japan's leading Kabuki stars of today.

Plays may go on all day, but normally just famous scenes will be performed. 'I was looking forward to that', shouts the audience as the actors freeze into a tableau.

Above Okumura Masanobu (active c.1700-64): *Scene from a Kabuki play*, 1744. The heroine (played by a man) is entering on the raised walkway ('flower walk') at the left: this enabled the audience to see the actors close-up. Two comic actors in exaggerated make-up can be seen at the centre of the stage. The audience of men and women in an Edo theatre would consist mainly of merchants, shopkeepers and craftsmen.

Left Toshusai Sharaku (active 1794-5): *Two actors in a play*, 1794. Both parts are played by men. Sharaku was famous for his theatrical prints.

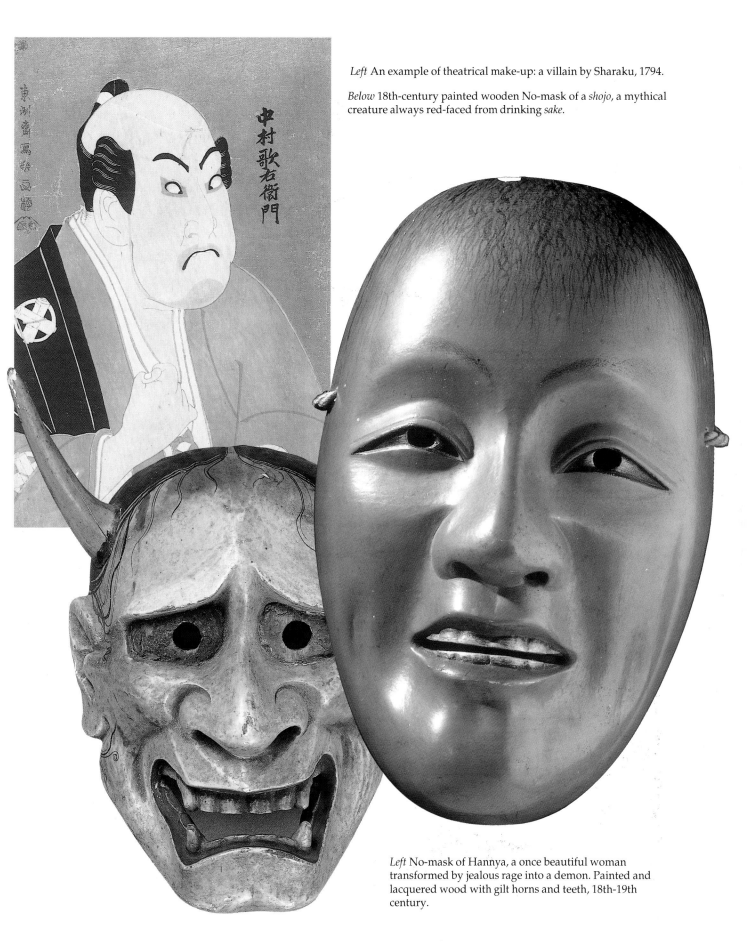

Left An example of theatrical make-up: a villain by Sharaku, 1794.

Below 18th-century painted wooden No-mask of a *shojo*, a mythical creature always red-faced from drinking *sake*.

Left No-mask of Hannya, a once beautiful woman transformed by jealous rage into a demon. Painted and lacquered wood with gilt horns and teeth, 18th-19th century.

Left Utagawa Kunisada (Toyokuni III, 1786-1864): *The Kabuki actor Koshiro Matsumoto.*

Opposite An actor performing at the Takigi No Theatre, Kyoto.

Below A modern performance of a Kabuki play in Kyoto.

ARCHITECTURE

The Buddhist ideal of 'economy of means' has permeated Japanese culture. Avoiding extravagant display and excessive detail and fostering a love of natural materials and forms in harmony with their surroundings are continuing themes in Japanese architecture.

Traditional Japanese houses, for example, are small, simple spaces of timber construction with a minimal amount of fixed furniture (to store bedding, clothing and crockery). Movable paper screens (*shoji*) separate spaces; painted and lacquered screens and kimonos on bamboo poles may also be used as room dividers. The floor of the room is made up of *tatami* floor mats, each 2 m by 1 m (6 ft x 3 ft). In this way, a house is built up organically from smaller units, unlike the Western tradition of designing a shell into which large items of furniture are then fitted, often therefore using space inflexibly and creating a cluttered interior. In Japan, Buddhist temple halls and imperial palaces are in their simplicity also quite unlike their Western counterparts from the Gothic or Baroque periods.

Western architecture came to Japan in the Meiji period: a college of architecture was founded at Tokyo University in 1874 by a pupil of the British architect William Burges. The first major Western architect to be influenced by Japanese architecture was Frank Lloyd Wright (1869-1959), who was greatly inspired by Japanese design at the Chicago World Fair in 1893 and then travelled to Japan in 1906. For him, 'Japanese art was nearer to the earth' than any other he knew, and this crucially influenced the thinking behind his earlier work with its emphasis on simplicity and the horizontal, as well as his later houses which appear to grow naturally out of the landscape. In 1916-22 he designed the Imperial Hotel in Tokyo in a mixture of Japanese and Western styles.

The first important building by a Japanese architect in the International Modern style was the Sogo Store in Osaka by Togo Murano (b.1891), opened in 1932. Japanese architects seized their opportunity following the 1923 earthquake which destroyed much of Tokyo, and their successors had the chance to recreate the city again after 1945. By 1953 the great German architect Walter Gropius (1883-1969) was writing: 'The one country which seems to have found a satisfactory modern architectural idiom is Japan.' He had trained Japanese architects at the Bauhaus in the 1930s; others worked for Le Corbusier (1887-1966), who designed the National Museum of Western Art in Tokyo (1959).

Foremost among this generation was Kenzo Tange (b.1913), who used the latest technology in steel and concrete for his 15,000-seat Olympic Gymnasium (1964) with its giant petal-like roof (p.54). His severe Peace Memorial at Hiroshima (1955) is still very Corbusian, but in the recent Sogetsu Art Centre he has created a Japanese-style interior landscape of steps and platforms inside an orthodox glazed box of a building. His Akasaka Prince Hotel in Tokyo (1983), however, could be anywhere in the world.

Under Tange's influence, the Metabolist Movement in Japan advocated a flexible architecture that stressed space rather than form and allowed for changes in function, unlike orthodox Western design. Tange has used the traditional wooden construction of post and beam, but in load-bearing concrete left rough, thus marrying Japanese simplicity with Le Corbusier's ideal of 'truth to materials'.

The interior of a Japanese house, with the characteristic *tatami* (woven straw) mats, *fusuma* (sliding paper doors) and a *tokonoma* (art alcove). Floor spaces are not cluttered with fixed furniture or chairs and tables, as in the West.

Arata Isozaki (b.1931), a former colleague of Tange's, is now Japan's best-known architect, particularly in the USA, where he has designed the new Museum of Contemporary Art in Los Angeles (1982-6), illustrated overleaf. Isozaki is extremely eclectic: Gunma Prefectural Museum of Fine Arts (1970-74) is a beautifully restrained, elegant piece of Modernist architecture that superficially could be in Paris or New York. Its aluminium grid structure, however, is derived from the Japanese tea house, just as Tange's concrete buildings derive from traditional timber houses. Isozaki's more recent work includes the Tsukuba Civic Centre (1983) for a technology new town, which quotes from great architects of the past (Michelangelo, Palladio and Ledoux) and from contemporaries like Richard Meier and Philip Johnson (see overleaf). It could thus be described as a kind of Japanese 'Post-Modernism': according to Charles Jencks, it 'conveys a very optimistic and innocent spirit of eclecticism'. This is even more apparent in the Okanoyama Graphic Art Museum (1982-3), with its use of bright colours (blue for the outside staircase and the tiled interior; yellow on the exterior walls) and its suggestion of classical columns and pediments. Like fashion, film or graphic design, therefore, 20th-century Japanese architecture is truly international.

Above The Horyuji Temple complex at Nara, founded in AD 607 and containing some of the oldest wooden buildings anywhere in the world, probably dating back to the later 7th century. From left to right can be seen the Buddha hall, the gatehouse and the pagoda.

Left Hiroshi Yoshida (1876-1950): *Himeji Castle, evening*, 1928. The most famous of all Japanese castles, dating mainly from the late 16th century, with thick stone walls to take account of the newly introduced European cannon. Known as the 'White Heron', Himeji was the seat of a daimyo as well as a fortress.

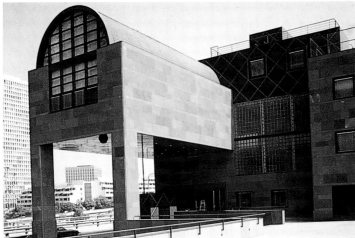

Above Arata Isozaki: Museum of Contemporary Art, Los Angeles, 1986. The library block, seen from the sculpture terrace.

Right Arata Isozaki: Tsukuba Civic Centre, Ibaraki. The main entrance of the Nova Hall, 1979-83, in the new Science City. A fine example of Japanese 'Post-Modernism', with references to classical and 18th-century European architecture.

Below right Kenzo Tange: National Gymnasium, Tokyo, 1961-4, built for the 1964 Olympic Games. A bold and sculptural use of modern technology for a 15,000-seat gymnasium and swimming pool.

GARDENS

Kyoto was the ancient imperial capital of Japan for over 1,000 years, until the 19th century. It was laid out on the model of a Chinese city and has over 1,500 temples. It also has some of the most celebrated Japanese gardens. In the pond garden of the Tenryuji Temple (completed in 1343) is an apparently natural arrangement of rocks. In fact they are carefully placed to suggest in miniature the ideal landscape of Song dynasty Chinese painting, and in particular the islands of the immortals, where fabulous mountains and flowers acted as a backcloth for everlasting life. Failing to discover these islands, Chinese emperors recreated them in their parks, and centuries later the Japanese did likewise.

The Buddhist vision of paradise as a palace by a lake was also conjured up by Chinese paintings and then recreated in Japanese gardens such as that of the Temple of the Golden Pavilion (Kinkakuji) in Kyoto (see p.57). The gilded pavilion was first built in 1397 as a retreat for the shogun. Previously, different vistas had opened up as one boated slowly around the lake. Now instead there was a fixed vantage point from the pavilion: the garden had become a painting. A sense of depth was contrived by positioning large rocks on the near side of the lake and small, dark, smooth ones on the other, with dwarf pines in the middle distance.

The garden of the Ryoanji Temple (completed in 1490), the most famous of all Zen gardens, is a 'dry-landscape' garden. It is enclosed by an earth wall and wooden veranda for viewing: there are no trees, flowers, grass or water, in deliberate contrast to the earlier lake-island garden beyond (see overleaf). Ryoanji embodies Zen

Meditating in the Zen garden at Ryoanji, Kyoto. With large numbers of tourists visiting daily, this is seldom the solitary experience that was originally intended.

Buddhist aesthetics seen also in monochrome ink painting and calligraphy, as well as new discoveries about suggesting perspective in gardens as in art, and a new mood of austerity following a civil war in which much of Kyoto was ruined. Patterns of white sand or gravel represent waves: they are remade daily by a monk with a wooden rake. Fifteen rocks, some of them edged with moss to look as ancient as possible, stand in the gravel. The largest group is at the front as viewed from the veranda, with progressively smaller rocks further away to make the space seem much larger than it really is. The rocks have been interpreted as mountains or clouds, or as a tigress leading her cubs across a stream. There is no fixed truth, for the essence of Zen is that we should take time from our busy lives and stop to contemplate in an atmosphere of peace and harmony. Zen gardens become what one writer has called 'a training ground for the spirit'.

Japanese ideas about gardens have

been enormously influential in the West, for instance in the ingenious design of small urban gardens to make them seem larger. Another famous example is the garden that the French painter Claude Monet (1840-1926) created at Giverny, inspired by his extensive collection of Japanese prints. He painted it repeatedly, notably in the 'Waterlilies' series, one of which is in the National Gallery, London. Waterlilies are a common feature of Japanese pool gardens.

Japan has also contributed many new plant species to the Western garden, particularly since 1860: these include many types of hydrangeas, camellias, chrysanthemums and magnolias.

Kado, 'the way of flowers', is better known in the West as *ikebana*, 'keeping flowers alive'. Originally a ritual performed by priests and then a competitive activity at court, it has become increasingly popular in Japan and throughout the world since the publication of Josiah Conder's *Floral Art of Japan* in 1899.

Left The Miyoshinji Zen Garden, Kyoto. Freshly raked patterns in the gravel may suggest waves breaking against rocks.

In Japanese culture, flowers are offered when the gods are invoked, for example to bless the rice harvest, at New Year or at a shrine. You do not, however, normally take flowers when visiting a Japanese family for dinner, for example. The choice and arrangement of flowers is extremely personal and disciplined by centuries of writing and teaching.

By the 16th century special rooms were designed in palaces for the viewing of flower arrangements to complement the flowerless gardens outside. For the Tea Ceremony one or two flowers only would be used. Three stems might symbolise Heaven, Earth and Man, and be pruned, trained and arranged at particular angles to create harmony and to express what was seen as the essence of each plant, as well as the season and the passage of time.

Just as a few flowers represent colourful nature in miniature, or small rocks mountains, so in *bonsai* dwarf trees represent the wildness of nature, inspired by the naturally dwarf trees that grow in windswept rocky crevices. Hardy trees such as cedar, maple and pine are trained to stay small and grow both outdoors and indoors, perhaps in the niche of honour on the veranda. In Japanese gardens, ikebana and bonsai we can see nature being reduced to a symbolic scale in a crowded country, and controlled so that contemplation of it may be as rewarding as possible.

Above The richly planted lake garden at Ryoanji, which contrasts strongly with the later Zen garden. The French artist Claude Monet was inspired to create a water garden like this at Giverny.

Right Varieties of bonsai, dwarf trees trained into symbolic shapes.

Left Ikebana is now enormously popular in the West, as in Japan.

Below The Golden Pavilion (Kinkakuji), Kyoto. Around a small lake are four and a half acres of exquisitely controlled mature trees, shrubs and rocks. The pavilion contains a small temple and rooms where the shogun could take tea, meditate and admire his art collection and the view outside.

MUSIC

When Buddhism came to Japan from China in the 7th and 8th centuries AD, the original *gagaku* ('elegant music') came too, and was established at court and in the temples. *Gagaku* is now a general term for early music and dance in Japan; music accompanied by dancing is specifically *bugaku* and predates both No and Kabuki. Today it is a rare art, still confined mainly to the Imperial household and a few shrines. The art of the musicians (who play from memory) has been handed down through a

Right A round-dance to celebrate the cherry blossom, from an early 17th-century six-fold screen (Kano School). A noble household sits watching the dancers in the courtyard of a Kyoto residence.

Below Francesca Harvey playing the *koto*. She studies in London with a Japanese teacher.

few families. Some of the repertoire has been rescored for modern symphony orchestra, and has inspired contemporary composers interested in the 'twelve-tone scale'.

Among the early musical instruments of Japan, the *biwa* is a kind of lute with four strings and the *koto* is a long instrument rather like a zither with thirteen strings. Playing the *koto* has long been considered an important accomplishment for young ladies, and today it is the most widely played of all the Japanese instruments, promoted by 20th-century governments as a national symbol. The *shakuhachi*, a reedless five-hole bamboo pipe, is the most familiar of Japanese wind instruments.

Many Western composers have been inspired by Japan. The opera *Madam Butterfly* (1904) by Giacomo

Left Seiji Ozawa conducting the Boston Symphony Orchestra. As well as conducting mainstream symphonic repertoire and recording operas such as *Carmen*, Ozawa has championed music by Takemitsu and other Japanese composers, and conducts Japan's leading orchestras.

Below A range of Japanese drums being played at the Japanese Festival in London.

A Zen priest playing the *shakuhachi* at the annual Japanese Festival in Battersea Park, London.

Puccini (1858-1924) is set in the 19th century and tells the story of an American officer who marries a Japanese geisha and then deserts her. He returns later to claim their child; as a result she commits suicide with her father's sword. Other European composers influenced by Japanese music and poetry include Olivier Messiaen (b.1908), Karlheinz Stockhausen (b.1928) in the 1960s, and John Cage (b.1912), who was particularly attracted to Zen ideas. The British composer Benjamin Britten (1913-76) adapted the music and performance rituals of No plays to Western chamber opera in *Curlew River* (1964). He had seen a 15th-century No play in Tokyo in 1956, which was a 'totally new operatic experience' for him. Britten translated the story to the East Anglian fens, kept the convention of the all male cast and used medieval English plainsong to maintain a sense of ritual.

One strongly Japanese feature of *Curlew River* is the prominent percussion. In recent years Japanese drummers have become well known in the West from extensive tours by the Kodo group, who create exciting 'walls of sound' on the *taiko* - traditional drums that increase in size up to a massive drum weighing 500 kg (1000 lbs) made from a hollow tree trunk and played with sticks the size of logs. The name Kodo derives from the heartbeat of a baby in its mother's womb.

Of contemporary Japanese composers, probably the best known in the West is Toru Takemitsu (b.1930), who is largely self-taught and who has straddled Japanese and Western music in his work. 'November Steps I' (1967), for example, is written for *biwa*, *shakuhachi* and orchestra.

FOOD AND DRINK

Kubo Shumman (1757-1820): *A party in the 'Four Seasons' restaurant at Nakazu on the Sumida River, Edo, c.*1786. A waitress brings in a tray of raw fish, while two geisha tune up their instruments.

Like so much in Japanese culture, many elements of Japanese cookery originated in China. Chinese Buddhism forbade meat-eating; sometimes the Japanese nobility cheated by hunting and eating wild boar, which they renamed 'mountain whale'. Most Japanese, however, adopted such early Chinese alternatives to meat as noodles, *sushi* (raw fish, pickled vegetables or seaweed with cold rice patties served with a sauce) and *miso* (a fermented soya bean paste often used in soups). Soya beans are as nutritious as red meat and very rich in iron. Buddhism also forbade strong seasonings such as onions, garlic or coriander, which might mask the true taste of the food. The Chinese and Japanese have developed alternative flavours such as sesame seeds, ginger, vinegar and grated white radish.

Like the Chinese, the Japanese still eat with chopsticks, and at home many still eat seated on the floor on *tatami* mats. After a break with China in the late 9th century, Japanese cookery developed a strong individuality. Rice plays a central role: for at least 2,000 years, for example, the national drink has been *sake*, a rice wine. Gods and heroes drank it in ancient myths, nobles and priests in the Middle Ages, and now it is even available from slot machines. Colourless like vodka, it can be drunk chilled in summer, or more usually warmed in small quantities so that the special aromas can be released.

Because three-quarters of Japan is mountainous, there is little room for growing arable crops, and so rice is intensively cultivated. Demand for it is so enormous that it costs at least three times as much as anywhere else. Japanese rice is short-grain, and eaten plain and slightly congealed so that it can be easily picked up with chopsticks. Each year the emperor ceremonially plants a paddy field of rice in the Imperial Palace. Most evening meals end with a bowl of rice and tea.

With the arrival of Europeans in the 16th century we have many first-hand accounts of Japanese food and drink:

'Fish, rootes and rice are their common junkets ... They have the same kyndes of beastes that we have, but they seldome eat anye fleshe ... They have strong wine and rack distilled of rice. They take great delighte in water mingled with a

Tiered picnic box in black lacquer with gold and shell decoration, late 17th century. Rice, fish, vegetables and pickles were packed into its separate compartments.

Octagonal nest of boxes with painting over red and gold lacquer, 17th century. The style is a mixture of Chinese art and that of the Ryukyu Islands, which were integrated into Japan only in the 19th century.

A smart vegetarian restaurant: the customers sit on *tatami* mats and eat from lacquer trays. A painted sliding screen and garden can be glimpsed at the back.

certain powder which is very pretiouse, which they call chai [tea].' (Leeming and Kohsaka, p.14.)

The Portuguese introduced new foods such as potatoes, corn and sugar, and new cooking ideas such as deep-frying in a batter of flour and egg. Deep-fried fish and vegetables in batter are called *tempura*, probably from the Portuguese word *tempora*, 'Friday', the day when fish is traditionally eaten in Catholic countries. A kind of sponge cake, also introduced from Europe, is called *kasutera*, from the word *castella*, and originates in Castille. Sugar and puddings have never become a central part of Japanese cuisine, but *tempura* is enormously popular today. So is *tonkatsu*, a Japanese version of schnitzel, breaded pork cutlets cut up into pieces manageable with chopsticks and served on a bed of shredded cabbage.

Not until the renewed contact with the West in the 19th century did meat-eating really catch on. In 1872 the emperor ate a completely European meal including beef. *Sukiyaki* is a popular dish of beef slices and vegetables, stir-fried in a pan at the table and then dipped into beaten egg on the plate. A particularly extraordinary and expensive delicacy is Kobe beef, from cattle that are massaged daily, rubbed down with *sake* and fed a special diet that includes beer. The meat is not only tender but aesthetically pleasing.

In Japan, cooking is an art and

younger generation may breakfast on 'morning' (coffee, toast and egg) and choose between noodles, a *sushi* bar or a McDonalds at lunchtime. What are considered by an outsider to be the generally bland flavours of Japanese food may now be supplemented by stronger tastes such as curry sauce.

Japanese food is generally quite healthy, using vegetable oil and few animal fats and dairy products; it is low in cholesterol and sugar, but high in salt. Vegetables are lightly

A typical Japanese lunchbox, where the textures and appearance (with plastic seaweed garnish) are as important as the taste.

eating often a ritual of order and harmony. There are strong aesthetic principles in ensuring fresh and contrasting colours as well as different flavours and textures at meals, and in giving a seasonal flavour with bamboo shoots in spring, chrysanthemum petals or red maple leaves for an autumn salad, and mushrooms floating in a soup to resemble autumn leaves.

The older generation may still eat less meat, and have a traditional breakfast with rice, fish, soya bean paste soup and some dried seaweed (seaweed is eaten in enormous quantities in Japan), while the

boiled to retain vitamins and colour, though polishing rice removes most of the Vitamin B.

As we have seen in other aspects of Japan today, food reflects the old and the new, the native and the foreign, and will no doubt continue to evolve while remaining distinctively Japanese.

CONCLUSION

Western artists continue to respond to Japan. As part of his 'attack on perspective' the British artist David Hockney (b.1937) became fascinated by Chinese landscape paintings and Japanese art. After a visit to Japan in 1971 he painted a blue acrylic *Mount Fuji and Flowers* (Metropolitan Museum of Art, New York) and the much more evocative *Japanese Rain on Canvas* (Private Collection). In 1983 he made photo collages of the Zen garden at Ryoanji. Conversely, the influence of Hockney's acrylic paintings of Californian swimming pools, 'Paper Pools' (1978), can be seen in the woodblock print *Summer Time* by the Japanese artist Satoru Matsushita.

Japanese responses to the cultural challenges of the later 20th century are inevitably diverse. Some artists are optimistic and draw strength from the past: 'If the craftsmen and designers of old Japan could create beauty with their materials, are we today to accept defeat when faced with ours?' asks the designer Hideyuki Oka (*How to Wrap Five More Eggs*, 1975).

Also looking back to Japan's past, however, conservatives like the novelist Yukio Mishima (from a former samurai family) may despair of 'the compromise culture of today' which in his view had gone soft after twenty years of peace 'when one may neither live beautifully nor die beautifully', and which was now dominated by 'expense account aristocrats, lionised baseball players and television stars'. Mishima

Satoru Matsushita (b.1957): *Summer Time - 2*, 1984.

committed suicide in 1970 by *seppuku,* after failing to rouse soldiers to revolt.

In this book we have seen contrasts between the extrovert and the ultra-refined, between traditional culture (much of it transformed from Chinese roots) and Western transplants, also transformed. As Soyetsu Yanagi, the friend of Bernard Leach, predicted in 1940, 'ours is destined to be the country where, as modern history shows, new and old, high and low, East and West, make their contact day by day' (Leach 1940, p.xvii).

Further Reading

ALEX, William, *Japanese Architecture*, London, Prentice-Hall, 1963.

ALLEN, Jeanne, *The Designer's Guide to Japanese Patterns*, 2 vols, London, Thames and Hudson, 1988-9.

AYERS, J. in Charleston, R.J. (ed.), *World Ceramics*, London, Hamlyn, 1977.

BANHAM, Reyner and SUZUKI, H., *Contemporary Architecture of Japan*, London, 1985.

BARR, Pat, *The Coming of the Barbarians*, London, Macmillan, 1967.

BARR, Pat, *Foreign Devils: Westerners in the Far East*, Harmondsworth, Penguin Education, 1970.

BIRDSALL, Derek (ed.), *The Living Treasures of Japan*, London, Wildwood House, 1973.

BROWN, Yu-Ying, *Japanese Book Illustration*, London, British Library, 1988.

CAREY, Frances and GRIFFITHS, Antony, *From Manet to Toulouse-Lautrec*, London, British Museum Publications, 1978.

COLLCUTT, M., JANSEN, M. and KAMAKURA, I., *Cultural Atlas of Japan*, Oxford, Phaidon, 1988.

EARLE, Joe (ed.), *Japanese Art and Design*, London, Victoria and Albert Museum, 1986.

FEWSTER, Stuart and GORTON, Tony, *Japan: From Shogun to Superstate*, Tenterden, Paul Norbury, 1988.

FLETCHER, Banister, *A History of Architecture*, ed. John Musgrove, 19th edn, London, Butterworth, 1987, chapters 22, 36 and 45.

HARDIE, P. and CONTE-HELM, M., *Japonisme*, Sunderland, Ceolfrith Press, 1986.

HARRIS, Victor, *Netsuke: The Hull Grundy Collection in the British Museum*, London, British Museum Publications, 1987.

HAYASHIYA, T. and S. and NAKAMURA, M., *Japanese Arts and the Tea Ceremony*, New York/Tokyo, Weatherhill/Heibonsha, 1974.

(Other titles in the Heibonsha Survey of Japanese Art include architecture, calligraphy, gardens and costume.)

HIBI, Sadao, *Japanese Detail*, 3 vols, London, Thames and Hudson, 1989.

HILLIER, Jack, *Hokusai*, Oxford, Phaidon, 1978.

HILLIER, Jack and SMITH, Lawrence, *Japanese Prints*, London, British Museum Publications, 1980.

HOOVER, Thomas, *Zen Culture*, London, Routledge and Kegan Paul, 1978.

HORMUTH, Norbert, *Hildebrand's Travel Guide: Japan*, Frankfurt, 1985.

IVES, Colta Feller, *The Great Wave: The Influence of Japanese Woodcuts on French Prints*, New York, Metropolitan Museum, 1974.

JACKSON, Paul, *Origami: A Complete Step by Step Guide*, London, Octopus, 1989.

KAHN, Herman, *The Emerging Japanese Superstate*, Harmondsworth, Penguin, 1973.

KATO, Shuichi, *Form, Style, Tradition: Reflections in Japanese Art and Society*, Tokyo, Kodansha, 1981.

KIROLLOS, Samira, *The Wind Children and Other Tales from Japan*, London, André Deutsch, 1989.

LANE, Richard, *Images from the Floating World*, Oxford, Oxford University Press, 1978.

LEACH, Bernard, *A Potter's Book*, 1940, reissued London, Faber and Faber, 1976.

LEACH, Bernard, *A Potter in Japan*, London, Faber and Faber, 1960.

LEEMING, Margaret and KOHSAKA, Mutsuko, *Japanese Cookery*, London, Century Hutchinson, 1984.

LOWE, John, *Japanese Crafts*, London, John Murray, 1983.

MILWARD, R.S., *Japan: The Past in the Present*, Tenterden, Paul Norbury, 1979.

MITSUKUNI, Y., IKKO, T. and TSUNE, S., *The Hybrid Culture: What Happened When East and West Met*, Tokyo, Mazda, 1984.

MOES, Robert, *Mingei: Japanese Folk Art*, Brooklyn Museum/Universe, 1985.

OKA, Hideyuki, *How to Wrap Five More Eggs: Traditional Japanese Packaging*, New York, Weatherhill, 1975.

PAINE, Robert Treat and SOPER, Alexander, *The Art and Architecture of Japan*, Pelican History of Art, 3rd edn, Harmondsworth, Penguin, 1981.

POPHAM, Peter, *The Insider's Guide to Japan*, London, Merehurst Press, 1987.

REISCHAUER, Edwin, *The Japanese*, Harvard, 1981.

SMITH, Lawrence, *The Japanese Print since 1900*, London, British Museum Publications, 1983.

SMITH, Lawrence, *Contemporary Japanese Prints*, London, British Museum Publications, 1985.

SMITH, Lawrence (ed.), *Ukiyoe: Images of Unknown Japan*, London, British Museum Publications, 1988.

SMITH, Lawrence and HARRIS, Victor, *Japanese Decorative Arts*, London, British Museum Publications, 1982.

SMITH, Lawrence, HARRIS, Victor and CLARK, Timothy, *Japanese Art: Masterpieces in the British Museum*, London, British Museum Publications, 1990.

SPARKE, Penny, *Japanese Design*, London, Michael Joseph, 1987.

STANLEY-BAKER, Joan, *Japanese Art*, London, Thames and Hudson, 1984.

TAMES, Richard, *The Japan Handbook: A Guide for Teachers*, Tenterden, Paul Norbury, 1981.

TURNBULL, S.R. *The Samurai: A Military History*, London, George Philip, 1977.

WHITFORD, Frank, *Japanese Prints and Western Paintings*, London, Studio Vista, 1977.

WICHMANN, Siegfried, *Japonisme*, London, Thames and Hudson, 1981.

Slides

A selection of slides of prints from the British Museum's collections is published by Icarus, 158 Boundaries Road, London SW12 8HG (Tel. 01-682 0900). The artists represented range from Moronobu (d.1695) to Reika Iwami (b.1927).

Video

Video Letter from Japan (TDK, 5-7 Queensway, Redhill, Surrey RH1 1YB) presents themes such as 'nobles and samurai' and 'living arts'.

Addresses

(See also R. Tames, *The Japan Handbook*, pp.119-22, for museums, shops, organisations and periodicals)

BRITISH MUSEUM EDUCATION SERVICE
London WC1B 3DG

BRITISH ORIGAMI SOCIETY
253 Park Lane
Poynton
Stockton
Cheshire SK12 1RH

JAPAN AIR LINES
8 Hanover Square
London W1

JAPAN BROADCASTING CORPORATION
London Bureau
43 Shoe Lane
London EC4

JAPAN INFORMATION CENTRE
(Embassy of Japan)
101-104 Piccadilly
London W1V 0AH

JAPAN NATIONAL TOURIST ORGANISATION
167 Regent Street
London W1

JAPAN TRADE CENTRE
Baker Street
London W1

JAPAN SOCIETY OF LONDON
630 Grand Buildings
Trafalgar Square
London WC2

LONDON UNIVERSITY, SCHOOL OF
ORIENTAL AND AFRICAN STUDIES
Extramural Division
Malet Street
London WC1

(NB Other universities with
major centres for Japanese
studies are Oxford, Cambridge
and Sheffield.)

THE URASENKE FOUNDATION
Tea Master: Michael A. Birch
28 Arlington Avenue
London N1

Photographic Acknowledgements

Robert Harding Picture
Library: pp.1 (Nigel Blythe), 4
(Robert McLeod), 16 above
(Carol Jopp), 38 below (Nigel
Blythe), 50 below and 52 (Carol
Jopp), 54 bottom (Sybil
Sassoon), 56-7 (water gardens
Christine Burton; ikebana
Bernadette Delaney). Graham
Harrison: pp.2-3 (street scene,
motorbike), 5 below, 51, 53
above, 55, 56 left, 61, 64. Greg
Irvine: pp.14-15, 24 left and
right, 37 (sword polisher), 41,
56 (bonsai), 58 below, 59 below
left, and right. Holburne
Museum and Crafts Study
Centre, Bath: pp.26, 30, 31
above. By courtesy of the
Trustees of the Victoria and
Albert Museum: pp.2 (dish), 36
(model samurai), 44 left.
Architectural Association: p.54
top and centre (Richard
Weston). Urasenke Foundation:
p.29. Clive Barda, London: p.59
above left. Keiko Hasegawa:
p.33 left. The Independent: p.46
left (Herbie Knott). Issey
Miyake: p.46 right (Tsutomu
Wakatsuki). Paul Jackson: p.25.

Index

Kites at the yearly Hamamatsu
Kite Festival.